# 11+ English

## Multiple-Choice Practice Paper
## Pack Two 11A

**Read these instructions before you start:**

- You have **50 minutes** to complete this paper.
- There are **50 questions** in this paper and each question is worth **one mark**.
- You may work out the answers in rough on a separate sheet of paper.
- Answers should be marked on the answer sheet provided, not on the practice paper.
- Mark your answer in the column marked with the same number as the question by drawing a firm line clearly through the box next to your answer.
- If you make a mistake, rub it out as completely as you can and mark you new answer. You should only mark one answer for each question.
- Work as quickly and carefully as you can.
- If you find a question difficult, do **NOT** spend too much time on it but move on to the next one.

# Moon Tuition
making the most of your potential

www.moontuition.co.uk

**Read this passage carefully and answer the questions that follow.**

<u>Cider with Rosie</u>

The village school at that time provided all the instruction we were likely to ask for. It was a small stone barn divided by a wooden partition into two rooms - The Infants and The Big Ones. There was one dame teacher and perhaps a young girl assistant. Every child in the valley went there, remained till he was fourteen years old, then was presented to the working field or
5  factory with nothing in his head but a few sayings, a jumbled list of wars, and a dreamy image of the world's geography. It seemed enough to get by with, in any case; and was one up on our poor old grandparents.

This school, when I came to it, was at its peak. It was packed to the walls with pupils. Wild boys and girls from miles around - from the outlying farms and half-hidden hovels way up at
10  the ends of the valley - swept down each day to add to our numbers, bringing with them strange oaths and odours, quaint garments and curious pies. They were my first amazed vision of any world outside the womanly warmth of my family; I didn't expect to survive it for long, and I was confronted with it at the age of four. The morning came, without any warning, when my sisters surrounded me, wrapped me in scarves, tied up my bootlaces, thrust a cap on my
15  head and stuffed a baked potato in my pocket. "What's this?" I asked. "You're starting school today." "I ain't. I'm stopping 'ome." "Now, come on, Loll. You're a big boy now." "I ain't." "You are." "Boo-hoo." They picked me up bodily, kicking and bawling, and carried me up the road. "Boys who don't go to school get put in boxes, and turn into rabbits, and get chopped up Sundays."

20  I felt this was overdoing it rather, but I said no more after that. I arrived at the school just three feet tall and fatly wrapped in my scarves. The playground roared like a rodeo, and the potato burned through my thigh. Old boots, ragged stockings, torn trousers and skirts, went skidding and skating around me. The rabble closed in; I was encircled, grit flew in my face like shrapnel. Tall girls with frizzled hair, and huge boys with sharp elbows, began to prod me with
25  hideous interest. They plucked at my scarves, spun me around like a top, twisted my nose, and stole my potato.

I was rescued at last by a gracious lady - the sixteen-year-old junior-teacher - who boxed a few ears and dried my face and led me off to The Infants. I spent that first day picking holes in paper, then went home in a smouldering temper. "What's the matter, Loll? Didn't he like
30  it at school, then?" "They never gave me the present!" "Present? What present?" "They said they'd give me a present." "Well, now, I'm sure they didn't." "They did! They said: 'You're Laurie Lee, ain't you? Well, you just sit there for the present.' I sat there all day but I never got it. I ain't going back there again!" But after a week I felt like a veteran and grew as ruthless as anyone else. Somebody had stolen my baked potato, so I swiped somebody else's apple.

**Reproduced from *Cider with Rosie* by Laurie Lee**

**Answer the following questions. You can look at the passage again to find the best answer and mark its letter on the answer sheet.**

**1**      Which of the following statements is TRUE?

      **A**   The village school only has one room.
      **B**   Students stayed in the village school until they were thirteen.
      **C**   Laurie Lee eventually settled into the school life.
      **D**   Laurie Lee was so excited on his first day to school.
      **E**   The teacher gave Laurie Lee a present.

**2**      Where did the children go after they left school when they were 14?

      **A**   Abroad.
      **B**   Working field or factory.
      **C**   Working field.
      **D**   Factory.
      **E**   University.

**3**      How old was Laurie Lee when he started to go to the school?

      **A**   4
      **B**   5
      **C**   6
      **D**   3
      **E**   7

**4**      What did Laurie Lee do to stop his sisters taking him to school?

      **A**   He begged.
      **B**   He cried and kicked.
      **C**   He threatened his sisters would turn into rabbits.
      **D**   He did nothing.
      **E**   He asked his mum for help.

**5**      What did Laurie Lee's sisters put in his pocket on his first day to school?

      **A**   A baked potato.
      **B**   Quaint garments.
      **C**   Curious pies.
      **D**   Sweets.
      **E**   Pocket money.

**6**   What did Laurie Lee do on the first day in school?

    **A**   He was reading books.
    **B**   He was playing with his friends in the playground.
    **C**   He was fighting with the boys.
    **D**   He was picking holes in paper.
    **E**   He was crying all day in school.

**7**   What figure of speech is "The playground roared like a rodeo" in line 21?

    **A**   metaphor
    **B**   simile
    **C**   hyperbole
    **D**   alliteration
    **E**   idiom

**8**   What does "ruthless" mean (line 33) ?

    **A**   friendly
    **B**   careless
    **C**   concerned
    **D**   cruel
    **E**   happy

**9**   Why did Laurie Lee go home in a smouldering temper?

    **A**   He didn't get a present from the school.
    **B**   He was too hungry.
    **C**   He didn't have a friend.
    **D**   He missed his mum so much.
    **E**   He was burnt by the potato.

**10**   What does "gracious" mean (line 27) ?

    **A**   strict
    **B**   loud
    **C**   angry
    **D**   quiet
    **E**   kind

**Answer the following questions about the types of words as they are used in the passage.**

**11**     What type of word is "provided" (line 1)?

    **A**  adjective
    **B**  adverb
    **C**  pronoun
    **D**  verb
    **E**  common noun


**12**     What type of word is "we" (line 1)?

    **A**  adjective
    **B**  adverb
    **C**  pronoun
    **D**  verb
    **E**  preposition


**13**     What type of word is "barn" (line 2)?

    **A**  adjective
    **B**  common noun
    **C**  pronoun
    **D**  proper noun
    **E**  preposition


**14**     What type of word is "wild" (line 8)?

    **A**  adjective
    **B**  common noun
    **C**  pronoun
    **D**  proper noun
    **E**  preposition

**15**  What type of word is "fatly" (line 21)?

    **A**    adjective
    **B**    abstract noun
    **C**    pronoun
    **D**    verb
    **E**    adverb

**16**  What type of word is "in" (line 29)?

    **A**    preposition
    **B**    abstract noun
    **C**    pronoun
    **D**    verb
    **E**    adverb

**17**  What type of word is "Laurie Lee"?

    **A**    common noun
    **B**    abstract noun
    **C**    pronoun
    **D**    proper noun
    **E**    adverb

**18**  What type of word is "sat"? (line 32)

    **A**    preposition
    **B**    verb
    **C**    pronoun
    **D**    proper noun
    **E**    adverb

**19**  What type of word is "veteran"? (line 33)

    **A**    preposition
    **B**    common noun
    **C**    pronoun
    **D**    proper noun
    **E**    adverb

**20**    What type of word is "swipe"? (line 34)

    **A**   verb
    **B**   common noun
    **C**   preposition
    **D**   proper noun
    **E**   adverb

---

In the following sentences there are some *spelling mistakes*. In each question there is either *one* mistake or *no* mistake. Find the group of words that contain the mistake and mark the group letter on your answer sheet. *If there is no mistake, mark the letter X.*

**21**    Jason recived his application from Reading School yesterday morning.
           A          B          C          D          X

**22**    They want to know what you think excelent customer service is.
           A          B          C          D          X

**23**    You can chose from a selection of hotels for your holiday.
           A          B          C          D          X

**24**    He was stoped by the police for speeding on M4.
           A          B          C          D          X

**25**    How did he build his company and become a very sucesful business man?
           A          B          C          D          X

**26**    This company is the bigest player in the mobile phone industry.
           A          B          C          D          X

**27**    She sat there quitely waiting for her grandfather to pick her up from the school.
           A          B          C          D          X

**28** Whether we go for a camping or not will depend on the whether.

    A        B        C        D        X

**29** They have provided all the equipments we need for the experement.

    A        B        C        D        X

**30** Unfortunatly, Mark won't be able to attend the meeting next Friday.

    A        B        C        D        X

---

In the following sentences there are some mistakes in the use of punctuation and capital letters. In each question there will be either *one* mistake or *no* mistake. Find the group of words that contain the mistake and mark the group letter on your answer sheet. *If there is no mistake, mark the letter X.*

**31** "Have you had your breakfast yet" asked Jim's mum.

    A        B        C    D        X

**32** This painting was bought by peter jones last month.

    A        B        C    D        X

**33** he leaned his back against the rail and blew a puff of smoke in the air.

    A        B        C        D        X

**34** Richards mother asked him if he wanted to go to the park.

    A        B        C    D        X

**35** Kevin asked Mark," Will you play football with me?

    A        B        C    D        X

**36** When the rain stopped we went out to play football again.

    A        B        C        D        X

**37**    At the age of 18, he started his first job as a waiter.
          A        B        C        D        X

**38**    All of a sudden he had a sharp pain in his stomach.
          A        B        C        D        X

**39**    I began to rub my eyes and pinch myself to see if it was a dream
          A        B        C        D        X

**40**    "He seems a lonely sad old man to me," said Andy.
          A        B        C        D        X

---

**Change the direct speech into indirect speech.**

**41**    Lily asked, 'Can I have a go?'
Lily asked _____ have a go.

    **A**   if she could
    **B**   she could
    **C**   if she can
    **D**   she can
    **E**   whether she can

**42**    Edward said, 'I don't want to play outside.'
Edward said _____ to play outside.

    **A**   I don't want
    **B**   he doesn't want
    **C**   he didn't want
    **D**   he hadn't want
    **E**   I didn't want

**43**   John said, 'I haven't seen her for a long time.'
John said _____her for a long time.

    **A**   I haven't seen
    **B**   he hadn't seen
    **C**   he hasn't seen
    **D**   I hadn't seen
    **E**   he didn't see

**44**   The headmaster said, 'There will be a new teacher joining tomorrow.'
The headmaster said _____a new teacher joining tomorrow.

    **A**   there will be
    **B**   there won't be
    **C**   there is
    **D**   there would be
    **E**   he will have

**45**   Phil asked, 'Can I start earlier?'
Phil asked _____start earlier.

    **A**   if I could
    **B**   he could
    **C**   if he can
    **D**   he can
    **E**   whether he could

**46**   'I am going to work,' said John.
John said _____to work .

    **A**   he will go
    **B**   he was going
    **C**   I am going
    **D**   he would have gone
    **E**   I was going

**47**   'It's a very beautiful park,' said Emma.
Emma said _____a very beautiful park.

    **A**   it was
    **B**   it is
    **C**   they were
    **D**   they are
    **E**   it will be

**48**   'When can you pick me up?'asked William.
William asked me _____pick him up.

    **A**   when I can
    **B**   when I could
    **C**   when he can
    **D**   when he could
    **E**   when I am going to

**49**   'Can you pass me that book please?'asked Alex.
Alex asked me _____him that book.

    **A**   whether I could pass
    **B**   if I can pass
    **C**   whether I can pass
    **D**   if I could have passed
    **E**   if I am willing to pass

**50**   'I haven't completed my homework yet,' said Benedict.
Benedict said _____his homework yet.

    **A**   I hadn't completed
    **B**   he hasn't completed
    **C**   he didn't completed
    **D**   he had completed
    **E**   he hadn't completed

# 11+ English

## Multiple-Choice Practice Paper
## Pack Two 11B

**Read these instructions before you start:**

- You have **50 minutes** to complete this paper.
- There are **50 questions** in this paper and each question is worth **one mark**.
- You may work out the answers in rough on a separate sheet of paper.
- Answers should be marked on the answer sheet provided, not on the practice paper.
- Mark your answer in the column marked with the same number as the question by drawing a firm line clearly through the box next to your answer.
- If you make a mistake, rub it out as completely as you can and mark you new answer. You should only mark one answer for each question.
- Work as quickly and carefully as you can.
- If you find a question difficult, do **NOT** spend too much time on it but move on to the next one.

# Moon Tuition
making the most of your potential

www.moontuition.co.uk

**Read this passage carefully and answer the questions that follow.**

Neanderthal large eyes 'caused their demise'

A study of Neanderthal skulls suggests that they became extinct because they had larger eyes than our species.

As a result, more of their brain was devoted to seeing in the long, dark nights in Europe, at the expense of high-level processing.

5   This ability enabled our species, Homo Sapiens, to fashion warmer clothes and develop larger social networks, helping us to survive the ice age in Europe.

The study is published in Proceedings of the Royal Society B Journal.

Neanderthals are a closely related species of human that lived in Europe from around 250,000 years ago. They coexisted and interacted briefly with our species until they went extinct about
10   28,000 years ago, in part due to an ice age.

The research team explored the idea that the ancestor of Neanderthals left Africa and had to adapt to the longer, darker nights and murkier days of Europe. The result was that Neanderthals evolved larger eyes and a much larger visual processing area at the back of their brains.

The humans that stayed in Africa, on the other hand, continued to enjoy bright and beautiful
15   days and so had no need for such an adaption. Instead, these people, our ancestors, evolved their frontal lobes, associated with higher level thinking, before they spread across the globe.

Eiluned Pearce of Oxford University decided to check this theory. She compared the skulls of 32 Homo sapiens and 13 Neanderthal skulls.

Ms Pearce found that Neanderthals had significantly larger eye sockets - on average 6mm
20   longer from top to bottom.

Although this seems like a small amount, she said that it was enough for Neanderthals to use significantly more of their brain to process visual information.

"Since Neanderthals evolved at higher latitudes, more of the Neanderthal brain would have been dedicated to vision and body control, leaving less brain to deal with other functions like
25   social networking," she told BBC News.

This is a view backed by Prof Chris Stringer, who was also involved in the research and is an expert in human origins at the Natural History Museum in London.

"We infer that Neanderthals had a smaller cognitive part of the brain and this would have limited them, including their ability to form larger groups. If you live in a larger group, you need a larger brain in order to process all those extra relationships," he explained.

The Neanderthals' more visually-focused brain structure might also have affected their ability to innovate and to adapt to the ice age that was thought to have contributed to their demise.

There is archaeological evidence, for example, that the Homo sapiens that coexisted with Neanderthals had needles which they used to make tailored clothing. This would have kept them much warmer than the wraps thought to have been worn by Neanderthals.

Prof Stringer said that all these factors together might have given our species a crucial advantage that enabled us to survive.

"Even if you had a small percent better ability to react quickly, to rely on your neighbours to help you survive and to pass on information - all these things together gave the edge to Homo sapiens over Neanderthals, and that may have made a difference to survival."

The finding runs counter to emerging research that Neanderthals were not the stupid brutish creatures portrayed in Hollywood films, but may well have been as intelligent as our species.

Oxford University's Prof Robin Dunbar, who supervised the study, said that the team wanted to avoid restoring the stereotypical image of Neanderthals.

"They were very, very smart, but not quite in the same league as Homo sapiens," he told BBC News.

"That difference might have been enough to tip the balance when things were beginning to get tough at the end of the last ice age," he said.

Up until now, researchers' knowledge of Neanderthals' brains has been based on casts of skulls. This has given an indication of brain size and structure, but has not given any real indication of how the Neanderthal brain functioned differently from ours. The latest study is an imaginative approach in trying to address this issue.

Previous research by Ms Pearce has shown that modern humans living at higher latitudes evolved bigger vision areas in the brain to cope with lower light levels. There is no suggestion though that their higher cognitive abilities suffered as a consequence.

Studies on primates have shown that eye size is proportional to the amount of brain space devoted to visual processing. So the researchers made the assumption that this would be true of Neanderthals.

**Reproduced from *BBC News***

**Answer the following questions. You can look at the passage again to find the best answer and make its letter on the answer sheet.**

1     Where did Neanderthals live around 250,000 years ago?

     **A**   Africa
     **B**   Asia
     **C**   Europe
     **D**   America
     **E**   Jupiter

2     When did Neanderthals go extinct?

     **A**   280,000 years ago
     **B**   250,000 years ago
     **C**   100,000 years ago
     **D**   28,000 years ago
     **E**   5000 years ago

3     Which one of the following statements is true?

     **A**   Neanderthals are closely related species of the humans that lived in Europe from around 250,00
     **B**   Neanderthals are aliens.
     **C**   Neanderthals are very stupid.
     **D**   Neanderthals have high-level processing.
     **E**   Neanderthals never coexisted with human species.

4     Why do Neanderthals have larger eyes than human species?

     **A**   Because they have to adapt to the completed social networks life.
     **B**   Because they can use less of their brain to process visual information.
     **C**   Because they have to use more brain to deal with social networking.
     **D**   Because they had to adapt to the longer, darker nights and murkier days of Europe.
     **E**   To survive in ice age.

**5**    How much longer are Neanderthals' eye sockets than human's from the top to the bottom?

    **A**    2mm
    **B**    60mm
    **C**    2cm
    **D**    6cm
    **E**    6mm

**6**    Who checked the theory that Neanderthals had larger eye sockets than our species?

    **A**    Oxford University
    **B**    Eiluned Pearce
    **C**    Prof Chris Stringer
    **D**    Prof Robin Dunbar
    **E**    Homo sapiens

**7**    How many more Homo sapiens' skulls than Neanderthal skulls did Ms Pearce use to check the theory that Neanderthals had larger eye sockets than our species??

    **A**    32
    **B**    19
    **C**    35
    **D**    13
    **E**    30

**8**    Which of the following statements is NOT true?

    **A**    Neanderthals have better social networking functions than humans.
    **B**    Neanderthals' smaller cognitive part of the brain limit them to form larger groups.
    **C**    Prof Chris Stringer is an expert in human origins at the Natural History Museum in London.
    **D**    Neanderthals have more visually-focused brain structure.
    **E**    Neanderthals have less advantage to survive in the ice age than humans.

**9**    What had been worn by Neanderthals from archaeological evidence?

    **A**    Tailored clothing.
    **B**    Leaves.
    **C**    Wraps.
    **D**    Animals' skins.
    **E**    Nothing.

**10**  Which one of the following might NOT have given human species a crucial advantage to survive in ice age?

    **A**  Better ability to react quickly.
    **B**  Larger social networking to rely on the neighbours to help them survive.
    **C**  High-level processing ability of brain.
    **D**  They evolved their frontal lobes associated with higher level thinking.
    **E**  They evolved larger eyes.

**11**  What has researchers' knowledge of Neanderthals' brains been based on up until now?

    **A**  Hollywood films.
    **B**  BBC news.
    **C**  Information from Proceedings of the Royal Society B Journal.
    **D**  Casts of Neanderthals' skulls.
    **E**  Nothing.

**12**  What has the research by Ms Pearce shown?

    **A**  Modern humans living at higher latitudes evolved smaller vision areas in the brain.
    **B**  Eye size is nothing to do with the amount of brain space devoted to visual processing.
    **C**  Modern humans living at higher latitudes evolved bigger vision areas in the brain.
    **D**  Neanderthals' skulls have given an indication of how exactly the Neanderthal brain work
    **E**  Homo sapiens have better visual processing than Neanderthals.

**Answer the following questions about the meanings of the words as they are used in the passage.**

**13**  What does 'coexisted' mean (line 9 )?

    **A**  didn't exist
    **B**  existed at the same time
    **C**  survived
    **D**  died
    **E**  involved in a battle

**14**   What does 'briefly' mean (line 9)?

    **A**   slowly
    **B**   suddenly
    **C**   for a short period
    **D**   heavily
    **E**   happily


**15**   What does 'murkier' mean (line 12)?

    **A**   clearer
    **B**   happier
    **C**   brighter
    **D**   darker, more unclear
    **E**   more cheerful


**16**   What does 'associated' mean (line 16)?

    **A**   connected
    **B**   evolved
    **C**   caused
    **D**   changed
    **E**   began


**17**   What do 'dedicated' mean (line 24)?

    **A**   hard working
    **B**   ideal
    **C**   meaningful
    **D**   successful
    **E**   set apart for a specific use or purpose


**18**   What does 'infer' mean (line 28 )?

    **A**   conclude
    **B**   make
    **C**   delay
    **D**   research
    **E**   study

**19**  What does 'demise' mean (line 32 )?

    **A**   appearance
    **B**   death
    **C**   intelligence
    **D**   body
    **E**   brain structure

**20**  What does 'latitude' mean (line 53 )?

    **A**   height
    **B**   length
    **C**   width
    **D**   thickness
    **E**   the angular distance north or south from the equator

**Answer the following questions about the types of words as they are used in the passage.**

**21**     Which of these is an abstract noun?

     **A**   study (line 1)
     **B**   Neanderthal (line 1)
     **C**   became (line 1)
     **D**   they (line 1)
     **E**   eyes (line 1)

**22**     Which of these is an adjective?

     **A**   result (line 3)
     **B**   brain (line 3)
     **C**   dark (line 3)
     **D**   seeing (line 3)
     **E**   Europe (line 3)

**23**     Which of these is a proper noun?

     **A**   Oxford University (line 17)
     **B**   theory (line 17)
     **C**   check (line 17)
     **D**   She (line 17)
     **E**   compared (line 17)

**24**     What type of words are the following?
      **clothes; ice; skulls; brain**

     **A**   adjectives
     **B**   adverbs
     **C**   pronouns
     **D**   common nouns
     **E**   prepositions

**25**   What type of words are the following?
**ability; intelligence; anger; sadness**

    **A**   verbs
    **B**   adjectives
    **C**   common nouns
    **D**   prepositions
    **E**   abstract nouns

**26**   What type of words are the following?
**it; they; she; he**

    **A**   common nouns
    **B**   pronouns
    **C**   proper nouns
    **D**   prepositions
    **E**   adverbs

**27**   What type of words are the following?
**warm; long; murky; dark**

    **A**   adverbs
    **B**   adjectives
    **C**   verbs
    **D**   pronouns
    **E**   abstract nouns

**28**   What type of words are the following?
**decide; dedicate; survive; compare**

    **A**   common nouns
    **B**   pronouns
    **C**   adverbs
    **D**   adjectives
    **E**   verbs

---

In the following sentences there are some *spelling mistakes*. In each question there will be either *one* mistake or *no* mistake. Find the group of words that contain the mistake and mark the group letter on your answer sheet. *If there is no mistake, mark the letter X.*

**29**   Schools minister David Laws said the programe would be completed on time.
          A          B          C    D      X

**30**   His teacher asked him to start his project immedietely.
          A      B      C      D      X

**31**   The condition of the school building was afecting teaching and learning.
          A      B      C      D      X

**32**   Councils are steping in to keep schools running while government struggles to get
          A          B          C

its act together.
          D      X

**33**   The condition of the building is getting in the way of provideing a good education.
          A      B      C      D   X

**34**   There will be a agreement on funding between the school and the council.
          A      B      C      D      X

**35**   This suggests that there house needs to be on the market for sale before July.
          A      B      C      D      X

---

In the following sentences there are some mistakes in the use of punctuation and capital letters. In each question there will be either *one* mistake or *no* mistake. Find the group of words that contain the mistake and mark the group letter on your answer sheet. *If there is no mistake, mark the letter X.*

**36**   we now know that Neanderthals were stocky with strong arms and hands.
          A      B      C      D      X

**37**  In 1909, excavations at La Ferrassie cave in the Dordogne unearthed the
     A           B           C

remains of a group of Neanderthals
             D                             X

**38**  One of the skeletons in that group was that of an adult male, given
          A           B           C

the name La Ferrassie 1.
             D                             X

**39**  La Ferrassie 1 is one of the most important discoveries made in the field of
          A           B           C

neanderthal research.
             D                             X

**40**  Much of La Ferrassie 1s frame was intact.
     A      B      C     D                             X

**41**  However, the thorax ribs pelvis and some spinal pieces were missing.
     A        B           C           D          X

**42**  British author Hilary mantel has been nominated for the Woman's Prize For Fiction.
        A           B           C             D      X

**43**  The Woman's Prize for Fiction is now in it's 18th year.
        A      B     C     D                         X

**44**  "We have to train our staff to be more efficient" said Mark.
        A       B       C        D               X

---

**In the following sentences choose the best word or words so that the sentences make sense and use the correct English.**

© Moon Tuition
www.moontuition.co.uk

**45**   The bones also provide clues with to in on upon the Neanderthal's lifestyle.

       A  B C D  E

**46**   The final stage of creating is creating creates created to create the replica was to add head.

       A     B     C     D     E

**47**   This may cast light on why our species survived but theres theirs their's their there didn't.

         A     B     C     D     E

**48**   There were others other's other the other others' clues to La Ferrassie 1's appearance.

       A     B     C     D     E

**49**   Adding the hair was a painstaking process of with in by for the model makers.

       A  B  C D E

**50**   They are designed and made according off of with to for the very latest research.

       A  B  C D E

# 11+ English

## Multiple-Choice Practice Paper
## Pack Two 11C

**Read these instructions before you start:**

- You have **50 minutes** to complete this paper.
- There are **50 questions** in this paper and each question is worth **one mark**.
- You may work out the answers in rough on a separate sheet of paper.
- Answers should be marked on the answer sheet provided, not on the practice paper.
- Mark your answer in the column marked with the same number as the question by drawing a firm line clearly through the box next to your answer.
- If you make a mistake, rub it out as completely as you can and mark you new answer. You should only mark one answer for each question.
- Work as quickly and carefully as you can.
- If you find a question difficult, do **NOT** spend too much time on it but move on to the next one.

# Moon Tuition
### making the most of your potential

www.moontuition.co.uk

© Moon Tuition
www.moontuition.co.uk

**Read this passage carefully and answer the questions that follow.**

<u>Eye of the Hurricane</u>

Mighty gusts of wind continued to shake the swamp shack where another violent gust of wind tore at the loosened corner of the roof.

"There it goes!" Tank exclaimed as the corner started to sag under the weight of rain.

A piece of corrugated sheeting sailed away and the corner collapsed inward, causing everyone
5  to scramble up and back as far away as possible.

"We're dead!" Garcia screamed. "We're all dead!"

"No, we're not!" the pilot cried. "The weight of the water on the roof caused that corner to collapse, but it'll soon drain off. Besides, I think I hear the storm easing off. So if that end of the roof holds up a little while longer, we can start for the cave."

10  Everyone except Garcia fell silent. He sank back down against the wall, closed his eyes and mumbled over and over, "Oh, God! Oh, God!"

It took a moment for Josh to realise that the man was praying in the only way he knew how.

Josh joined the others in listening hopefully as the rain and wind slowly faded away. Falling rain from the collapsed end of the roof eased off too, but there was so much water on the floor
15  that everyone's feet were wet.

Finally, Eddie stood up. "The eye of the hurricane is almost here," he announced. "We'll have about fifteen minutes to reach the cave before the back side of the storm starts..."

"I'm getting out of here now!" Frank interrupted, hoisting himself to his feet and pulling on his raincoat. "Come on, Garcia. If you want to live through this thing, you've got to help yourself."
20  "Wait!" the pilot cried, but the big poacher yanked the door open and plunged through it.

The wind and rain gushed into the tiny room, making it rock so hard Josh feared it would blow off the foundation. The force of the wind made him turn his head momentarily. When he looked again, Frank and Garcia were gone, leaving their backpacks behind.

Eddie said sadly, "They shouldn't have done that."

25  A few minutes later, Eddie decided it was safe to head for the cave. Everyone stood and stepped outside.

Now only light rain fell, unlike the blinding downpour of the past few hours. The incredible gusting winds had completely died down. Josh squinted at the sky. The dark clouds warned that this was only a momentary lull. Greater natural fury was coming.

30     "Fifteen minutes before the eye passes," Eddie warned. "We'd better be in the cave before then, or we may not be so lucky when the back side of the storm hits."

It was very hard going because the hillside was slick, and there were countless downed trees, uprooted shrubs and mud slides everywhere. Still, Josh was so glad to be out of the shack that he didn't really mind.

35     Maybe Dad and Dr Nakamura are in the cave, Josh thought, ignoring the mud that weighted down his shoes. He hurried through the hurricane's eye in renewed hope.

**Reproduced from *Eye of the Hurricane* by Lee Roddy**

**Answer the following questions. You can look at the passage again to find the best answer and mark its letter on the answer sheet.**

**1**    What does "Mighty" mean? (line 1)

    **A**    powerful
    **B**    strength
    **C**    small
    **D**    lack
    **E**    slight

**2**    What type of word is "tore"? (line 2)

    **A**    noun
    **B**    verb
    **C**    adjective
    **D**    pronoun
    **E**    adverb

**3**    What does "exclaimed" mean?(line 3)

    **A**    escape
    **B**    jump
    **C**    run
    **D**    request
    **E**    shout

**4**    Who said "We're all dead!" when the corner of the roof collapsed inward?

    **A**    Frank
    **B**    Tank
    **C**    Garcia
    **D**    Josh
    **E**    Eddie

**5**   What does "mumbled" mean? (line 11)

    **A**   shouted
    **B**   chewed
    **C**   cried
    **D**   spoke in a low voice
    **E**   thought

**6**   Who is the "big poacher"?(line20)

    **A**   pilot
    **B**   Eddie
    **C**   Frank
    **D**   Josh
    **E**   Garcia

**7**   What type of word is "tiny" (line 21) ?

    **A**   Pronoun.
    **B**   Abstract noun.
    **C**   Proper noun.
    **D**   Verb.
    **E**   Adjective.

**8**   What type of word is "foundation" (line 22)?

    **A**   Abstract noun.
    **B**   Common noun.
    **C**   Preposition.
    **D**   Verb.
    **E**   Adjective.

**9**   What does "momentarily" mean (line 22)?

    **A**   a long time
    **B**   easily
    **C**   hardly
    **D**   temporarily
    **E**   sufficiently

**10**     What type of word is "Eddie" (line 30)?

      **A**    Proper noun.
      **B**    Abstract noun.
      **C**    Preposition.
      **D**    Verb.
      **E**    Adjective.

**11**     What does "slick" mean (line 32)?

      **A**    tired
      **B**    slice
      **C**    slippery
      **D**    move
      **E**    difficult

**12**     What does "countless" mean? (line 32)

      **A**    few
      **B**    slim
      **C**    rough
      **D**    number
      **E**    too many

**13**     Who left their backpacks behind and went to the cave before Eddie?

      **A**    Nobody
      **B**    Only Frank
      **C**    Garcia and Frank
      **D**    Josh
      **E**    Only Garcia

**14**     Why do you think Josh hurried through the hurricane's eye in renewed hope? (line 35)

      **A**    Because he thought his dad and Dr Nakamura were in the cave.
      **B**    Because he thought the hurricane would stop very soon.
      **C**    Because the hurricane stopped.
      **D**    Because someone would come to rescue him.
      **E**    Because he thought the hurricane was not as hard as expected.

**Change the following active sentences to passive sentences.**

**15**  Jack kicked the football.

   **A**  The football was kicked by Jack.
   **B**  The football is kicked by Jack.
   **C**  Jack was kicking the football.
   **D**  The football was kicked by him.
   **E**  The football is kicked by him.

**16**  Nathan left the key on the table.

   **A**  The key is left on the table by Nathan.
   **B**  The key was left on the table by Nathan.
   **C**  Nathan was left the key on the table.
   **D**  Nathan was leaving the key on the table.
   **E**  There was the key on the table left by Nathan.

**17**  The dog knocked over the bottle.

   **A**  The bottle is knocked over by the cat.
   **B**  The bottle was knocked over by the cat.
   **C**  The dog was knocked by the bottle.
   **D**  The bottle was knocked over by the dog.
   **E**  The bottle knocked over by the dog.

---

**Change the following passive sentences to active sentences.**

**18**  The window was smashed by Jason.

   **A**  He smashed the window.
   **B**  Jason has smashed the window..
   **C**  Jason smashed the window.
   **D**  Jason had smashed the window.
   **E**  Jason smashes the window..

**19**   The tree was pushed over by John.

    **A**   John is pushing over the tree.
    **B**   John pushed over the tree.
    **C**   The tree pushed over by John.
    **D**   He pushed over the tree.
    **E**   John was pushing over the tree.

**Change the direct speech into indirect speech.**

**20**   'It's very cold.' said Emma.
Emma said_____.

    **A**   it is very cold.
    **B**   it is not very cold.
    **C**   it was very cold.
    **D**   it is not warm.
    **E**   it was not warm.

**21**   'I am very exhausted.'said Sam.
Sam said he _____very exhausted.

    **A**   was
    **B**   is
    **C**   have been
    **D**   had been
    **E**   will be

**22**   'Can you get me a drink please?'asked Beck.
Beck asked if I _____a drink.

    **A**   can get me
    **B**   will get him
    **C**   could get him
    **D**   could have got me
    **E**   had got him

**23**     'We're going to the zoo.' said Lara.
Lara said they _____the zoo.

    **A**   will go to
    **B**   would go to
    **C**   went to
    **D**   were going to
    **E**   had gone to

**24**     'The books haven't arrived yet.' said Saul.
Saul said the books _____yet.

    **A**   hadn't arrived
    **B**   would not have arrived
    **C**   didn't arrive
    **D**   had arrived
    **E**   hasn't arrived

**25**     'Have you been to Cambridge?' asked Lewis.
Lewis asked me_____Cambridge.

    **A**   I went to
    **B**   I had been to
    **C**   if I had been to
    **D**   whether I went to
    **E**   if I have been to

---

**In the following sentences there are some *spelling mistakes*. In each question there will be either *one* mistake or *no* mistake. Find the group of words that contain the mistake and mark the group letter on your answer sheet. *If there is no mistake, mark the letter X.***

**26**     I need to check my calandar first before I - make an appointment.
        A         B         C         D         X

**27**     It allows the child to talk about things that happened in the past.
        A         B         C         D         X

**28** This is just something you are giveing her to play with for a while.
   A    B    C    D                                          X

**29** Allow the child time to act on the object in whatever way he choses.
   A    B    C    D                                          X

**30** Not all children respond immedietely when presented with an object.
   A    B    C    D                                          X

**31** After completing the activity, the child droped the object in the "finished" basket.
   A    B    C    D                                          X

**32** It is important to build in suficient wait time for the child to respond.
   A    B    C    D                                          X

**33** Their must have been an accident on M4.
   A    B    C    D                                          X

**34** Edward's firend went to the cinema with him last Saturday.
   A    B    C    D                                          X

**35** The new school is very proud of its reputation.
   A    B    C    D                                          X

In the following sentences there are some mistakes in the use of punctuation and capital letters. In each question there will be either *one* mistake or *no* mistake. Find the group of words that contain the mistake and mark the group letter on your answer sheet. *If there is no mistake, mark the letter X.*

**36**  After stealing the car the thief lost his way and ended up in the chief
          A                    B                        C

constable's garage.
          D                                                                                    X

**37**  We decided to visit Spain, Greece, Portugal and italy's mountains.
                          A          B              C              D                         X

**38**  That short boy, Jimmy's brother is this month's winner.
                    A            B            C          D                               X

**39**  The beaches in Cornwall are warm sandy and spotlessly clean.

                A              B              C                    D                        X

**40**  Lihi left her books in the caretakers cupboard.
              A      B        C          D                                                 X

**41**  Eddie asked Nathan, " When will you go to the library"
                A                    B              C          D                          X

**42**  "It is never going to work!" shouted John
              A          B        C          D                                             X

In the following sentences choose the best word or words so that the sentences make sense and use the correct English.

**43**  I don't know why its it's it has it' is it had difficult for you to understand.
                          A    B    C    D    E

**44**  You need to improve improving improved have improved been improving your French.
      A         B         C            D               E

**45**  Do you think their is their are there are they is there is a quick way to get here?
      A         B         C         D         E

**46**  As you go through off away about on your life, there will be various challenges.
      A      B     C     D     E

**47**  I brought the washing in so because even if such that but it was raining.
      A        B        C         D         E

**48**  We went fishing so as although and so that it was an awful day.
      A B      C      D       E

**49**  It seemed like the cake was given to everyone accept apart with but because me.
                                          A       B       C    D    E

**50**  He loves be listening to listening listened have listened listening to classical music.
      A              B          C           D               E

# Moon Tuition
making the most of your potential

## 11+ English Multiple-Choice Answer Sheet 11A

Pupil's Name

Date of Test

School's Name

### DATE OF BIRTH

| Day | | Month | | Year | |
|-----|-----|-------|-----|------|-----|
| [0] | [0] | January | ▭ | 2000 | ▭ |
| [1] | [1] | February | ▭ | 2001 | ▭ |
| [2] | [2] | March | ▭ | 2002 | ▭ |
| [3] | [3] | April | ▭ | 2003 | ▭ |
| | [4] | May | ▭ | 2004 | ▭ |
| | [5] | June | ▭ | 2005 | ▭ |
| | [6] | July | ▭ | 2006 | ▭ |
| | [7] | August | ▭ | 2007 | ▭ |
| | [8] | September | ▭ | 2008 | ▭ |
| | [9] | October | ▭ | 2009 | ▭ |
| | | November | ▭ | 2010 | ▭ |
| | | December | ▭ | 2011 | ▭ |

**Please mark like this** ⟵

### PUPIL NUMBER

| [0] | [0] | [0] | [0] | [0] | [0] |
|-----|-----|-----|-----|-----|-----|
| [1] | [1] | [1] | [1] | [1] | [1] |
| [2] | [2] | [2] | [2] | [2] | [2] |
| [3] | [3] | [3] | [3] | [3] | [3] |
| [4] | [4] | [4] | [4] | [4] | [4] |
| [5] | [5] | [5] | [5] | [5] | [5] |
| [6] | [6] | [6] | [6] | [6] | [6] |
| [7] | [7] | [7] | [7] | [7] | [7] |
| [8] | [8] | [8] | [8] | [8] | [8] |
| [9] | [9] | [9] | [9] | [9] | [9] |

### SCHOOL NUMBER

| [0] | [0] | [0] | [0] | [0] | [0] | [0] |
|-----|-----|-----|-----|-----|-----|-----|
| [1] | [1] | [1] | [1] | [1] | [1] | [1] |
| [2] | [2] | [2] | [2] | [2] | [2] | [2] |
| [3] | [3] | [3] | [3] | [3] | [3] | [3] |
| [4] | [4] | [4] | [4] | [4] | [4] | [4] |
| [5] | [5] | [5] | [5] | [5] | [5] | [5] |
| [6] | [6] | [6] | [6] | [6] | [6] | [6] |
| [7] | [7] | [7] | [7] | [7] | [7] | [7] |
| [8] | [8] | [8] | [8] | [8] | [8] | [8] |
| [9] | [9] | [9] | [9] | [9] | [9] | [9] |

1. A B C D E
2. A B C D E
3. A B C D E
4. A B C D E
5. A B C D E
6. A B C D E
7. A B C D E
8. A B C D E
9. A B C D E
10. A B C D E
11. A B C D E
12. A B C D E
13. A B C D E
14. A B C D E
15. A B C D E
16. A B C D E
17. A B C D E
18. A B C D E
19. A B C D E
20. A B C D E
21. A B C D E
22. A B C D E
23. A B C D X
24. A B C D X
25. A B C D X
26. A B C D X
27. A B C D X
28. A B C D X
29. A B C D X
30. A B C D X
31. A B C D X
32. A B C D X
33. A B C D X
34. A B C D X
35. A B C D X
36. A B C D X
37. A B C D X
38. A B C D X
39. A B C D X
40. A B C D E
41. A B C D E
42. A B C D E
43. A B C D E
44. A B C D E
45. A B C D E
46. A B C D E
47. A B C D E
48. A B C D E
49. A B C D E
50. A B C D E

# Moon Tuition
making the most of your potential

# 11+ English Multiple-Choice Answer Sheet 11B

Pupil's Name

School's Name

Date of Test

**Please mark like this** ⟵

| PUPIL NUMBER | SCHOOL NUMBER |
|---|---|

Pupil Number columns:
[0] [0] [0] [0] [0] [0]
[1] [1] [1] [1] [1] [1]
[2] [2] [2] [2] [2] [2]
[3] [3] [3] [3] [3] [3]
[4] [4] [4] [4] [4] [4]
[5] [5] [5] [5] [5] [5]
[6] [6] [6] [6] [6] [6]
[7] [7] [7] [7] [7] [7]
[8] [8] [8] [8] [8] [8]
[9] [9] [9] [9] [9] [9]

School Number columns:
[0] [0] [0] [0] [0] [0] [0]
[1] [1] [1] [1] [1] [1] [1]
[2] [2] [2] [2] [2] [2] [2]
[3] [3] [3] [3] [3] [3] [3]
[4] [4] [4] [4] [4] [4] [4]
[5] [5] [5] [5] [5] [5] [5]
[6] [6] [6] [6] [6] [6] [6]
[7] [7] [7] [7] [7] [7] [7]
[8] [8] [8] [8] [8] [8] [8]
[9] [9] [9] [9] [9] [9] [9]

| DATE OF BIRTH | | |
|---|---|---|
| **Day** | **Month** | **Year** |
| [0] [0] | January | 2000 |
| [1] [1] | February | 2001 |
| [2] [2] | March | 2002 |
| [3] [3] | April | 2003 |
| [4] | May | 2004 |
| [5] | June | 2005 |
| [6] | July | 2006 |
| [7] | August | 2007 |
| [8] | September | 2008 |
| [9] | October | 2009 |
| | November | 2010 |
| | December | 2011 |

**1** A B C D E
**2** A B C D E
**3** A B C D E
**4** A B C D E
**5** A B C D E
**6** A B C D E
**7** A B C D E
**8** A B C D E
**9** A B C D E

**10** A B C D E
**11** A B C D E
**12** A B C D E
**13** A B C D E
**14** A B C D E
**15** A B C D E
**16** A B C D E
**17** A B C D E
**18** A B C D E

**19** A B C D E
**20** A B C D E
**21** A B C D E
**22** A B C D E
**23** A B C D E
**24** A B C D E
**25** A B C D E
**26** A B C D X
**27** A B C D X

**28** A B C D X
**29** A B C D X
**30** A B C D X
**31** A B C D X
**32** A B C D X
**33** A B C D X
**34** A B C D X
**35** A B C D X
**36** A B C D X

**37** A B C D X
**38** A B C D X
**39** A B C D X
**40** A B C D X
**41** A B C D X
**42** A B C D X
**43** A B C D E
**44** A B C D E
**45** A B C D E

**46** A B C D E
**47** A B C D E
**48** A B C D E
**49** A B C D E
**50** A B C D E

# Moon Tuition
*making the most of your potential*

## 11+ English Multiple-Choice Answer Sheet 11C

Pupil's Name

School's Name

Date of Test

Please mark
like this ←⌐

### PUPIL NUMBER

| | | | | | |
|---|---|---|---|---|---|
| [0] | [0] | [0] | [0] | [0] | [0] |
| [1] | [1] | [1] | [1] | [1] | [1] |
| [2] | [2] | [2] | [2] | [2] | [2] |
| [3] | [3] | [3] | [3] | [3] | [3] |
| [4] | [4] | [4] | [4] | [4] | [4] |
| [5] | [5] | [5] | [5] | [5] | [5] |
| [6] | [6] | [6] | [6] | [6] | [6] |
| [7] | [7] | [7] | [7] | [7] | [7] |
| [8] | [8] | [8] | [8] | [8] | [8] |
| [9] | [9] | [9] | [9] | [9] | [9] |

### SCHOOL NUMBER

| | | | | | | |
|---|---|---|---|---|---|---|
| [0] | [0] | [0] | [0] | [0] | [0] | [0] |
| [1] | [1] | [1] | [1] | [1] | [1] | [1] |
| [2] | [2] | [2] | [2] | [2] | [2] | [2] |
| [3] | [3] | [3] | [3] | [3] | [3] | [3] |
| [4] | [4] | [4] | [4] | [4] | [4] | [4] |
| [5] | [5] | [5] | [5] | [5] | [5] | [5] |
| [6] | [6] | [6] | [6] | [6] | [6] | [6] |
| [7] | [7] | [7] | [7] | [7] | [7] | [7] |
| [8] | [8] | [8] | [8] | [8] | [8] | [8] |
| [9] | [9] | [9] | [9] | [9] | [9] | [9] |

### DATE OF BIRTH

| Day | Month | Year |
|---|---|---|
| [0] [0] | January ⌐ | 2000 ⌐ |
| [1] [1] | February ⌐ | 2001 ⌐ |
| [2] [2] | March ⌐ | 2002 ⌐ |
| [3] [3] | April ⌐ | 2003 ⌐ |
| [4] | May ⌐ | 2004 ⌐ |
| [5] | June ⌐ | 2005 ⌐ |
| [6] | July ⌐ | 2006 ⌐ |
| [7] | August ⌐ | 2007 ⌐ |
| [8] | September ⌐ | 2008 ⌐ |
| [9] | October ⌐ | 2009 ⌐ |
| | November ⌐ | 2010 ⌐ |
| | December ⌐ | 2011 ⌐ |

**1** A B C D E
**2** A B C D E
**3** A B C D E
**4** A B C D E
**5** A B C D E
**6** A B C D E
**7** A B C D E
**8** A B C D E
**9** A B C D E

**10** A B C D E
**11** A B C D E
**12** A B C D E
**13** A B C D E
**14** A B C D E
**15** A B C D E
**16** A B C D E
**17** A B C D E
**18** A B C D E

**19** A B C D E
**20** A B C D E
**21** A B C D E
**22** A B C D E
**23** A B C D E
**24** A B C D E
**25** A B C D E
**26** A B C D X
**27** A B C D X

**28** A B C D X
**29** A B C D X
**30** A B C D X
**31** A B C D X
**32** A B C D X
**33** A B C D X
**34** A B C D X
**35** A B C D X
**36** A B C D X

**37** A B C D X
**38** A B C D X
**39** A B C D X
**40** A B C D X
**41** A B C D X
**42** A B C D X
**43** A B C D E
**44** A B C D E
**45** A B C D E

**46** A B C D E
**47** A B C D E
**48** A B C D E
**49** A B C D E
**50** A B C D E

# 11+ English

## Answer Key for
## Multiple-Choice Practice Papers
## Pack Two

### Read these instructions before you start marking:

- Only the answers given are allowed.
- One mark should be given for each correct answer.
- Do not deduct marks for the wrong answers.

# Moon Tuition
making the most of your potential

www.moontuition.co.uk

17143434R00026

Printed in Great Britain
by Amazon